Spring into Mental Maths with CGP!

The daffodils are out, lambs are in the fields, the days are getting longer... it must be time for some Mental Maths Daily Practice from CGP!

This brilliant book covers a huge range of skills from the Year 3 curriculum, with a page of practice for every day of the spring term.

And it doesn't stop there — this treasure trove of examples and colourful pictures will keep pupils engaged in class and at home. Spring-tastic!

What CGP is all about

Our sole aim here at CGP is to produce the highest quality books — carefully written, immaculately presented and dangerously close to being funny.

Then we work our socks off to get them out to you — at the cheapest possible prices.

Contents

☑ Use the tick boxes to help keep a record of which tests have been attempted.

Week 1
- ☐ Day 1 1
- ☐ Day 2 2
- ☐ Day 3 3
- ☐ Day 4 4
- ☐ Day 5 5

Week 2
- ☐ Day 1 6
- ☐ Day 2 7
- ☐ Day 3 8
- ☐ Day 4 9
- ☐ Day 5 10

Week 3
- ☐ Day 1 11
- ☐ Day 2 12
- ☐ Day 3 13
- ☐ Day 4 14
- ☐ Day 5 15

Week 4
- ☐ Day 1 16
- ☐ Day 2 17
- ☐ Day 3 18
- ☐ Day 4 19
- ☐ Day 5 20

Week 5
- ☐ Day 1 21
- ☐ Day 2 22
- ☐ Day 3 23
- ☐ Day 4 24
- ☐ Day 5 25

Week 6
- ☐ Day 1 26
- ☐ Day 2 27
- ☐ Day 3 28
- ☐ Day 4 29
- ☐ Day 5 30

Week 7
- ☐ Day 1 31
- ☐ Day 2 32
- ☐ Day 3 33
- ☐ Day 4 34
- ☐ Day 5 35

Week 8
- ☐ Day 1 36
- ☐ Day 2 37
- ☐ Day 3 38
- ☐ Day 4 39
- ☐ Day 5 40

Week 9

- ☑ Day 1 41
- ☑ Day 2 42
- ☑ Day 3 43
- ☑ Day 4 44
- ☑ Day 5 45

Week 10

- ☑ Day 1 46
- ☑ Day 2 47
- ☑ Day 3 48
- ☑ Day 4 49
- ☑ Day 5 50

Week 11

- ☑ Day 1 51
- ☑ Day 2 52
- ☑ Day 3 53
- ☑ Day 4 54
- ☑ Day 5 55

Week 12

- ☑ Day 1 56
- ☑ Day 2 57
- ☑ Day 3 58
- ☑ Day 4 59
- ☑ Day 5 60

Answers 61

Published by CGP

ISBN: 978 1 78908 772 7

Editors: Katherine Faudemer, Katie Fernandez, Tamara Sinivassen and George Wright

With thanks to Gail Renaud and Glenn Rogers for the proofreading.

With thanks to Lottie Edwards for the copyright research.

Clipart from Corel®

1 pence coin © iStock.com/coopder1
2 pence coin © iStock.com/peterspiro
5p and 50 pence coin © iStock.com/duncan1890
10 pence coin © iStock.com/john shepherd
20 pence coin © iStock.com/Jaap2

Printed by W&G Baird Ltd, Antrim.
Based on the classic CGP style created by Richard Parsons.

Text, design, layout and original illustrations © Coordination Group Publications Ltd. (CGP) 2021
All rights reserved.

Photocopying this book is not permitted, even if you have a CLA licence.
Extra copies are available from CGP with next day delivery • 0800 1712 712 • www.cgpbooks.co.uk

How to Use this Book

- This book contains 60 daily practice tests.

- We've split them into 12 sections — that's roughly one for each week of the Year 3 spring term.

- Each week is made up of 5 tests, so there's one for every school day of the term (Monday – Friday).

- Each test should take about 10 minutes to complete.

- Pupils should aim to do their working in their heads, without writing anything down.

- The tests contain a mix of Mental Maths topics from Year 3. New Year 3 topics are gradually introduced as you go through the book.

- The tests increase in difficulty as you progress through the term.

- Each test looks something like this:

The Week and the Day of the test are shown at the top of the page.

The instruction the pupil needs to follow is in the box at the top of the page.

There's an example at the top of the page. The correct answer is shown in red. Talk the pupil through the instruction and the example so they know what to do.

There are between 4 and 14 questions for the pupil to answer.

There's a score box at the bottom of the test. Use this to keep track of how well the pupil has done.

Week 1 — Day 1

Fill in the boxes with the missing numbers in the sequence.

| 0 | 100 | **200** | 300 | 400 | **500** |

1) | 200 | 300 | 400 | 500 | | |

2) | | | 700 | 800 | 900 | 1000 |

3) | 100 | | 300 | | 500 | 600 |

4) | | 400 | | 200 | 100 | 0 |

5) | 900 | 800 | | | 500 | 400 |

6) | 400 | 500 | 600 | | | 900 |

7) | 1100 | 1000 | 900 | 800 | | |

8) | 700 | 800 | 900 | | 1100 | |

Today I scored ☐ out of 8.

Week 1 — Day 2

The table shows the number of different types of pizza sold each day. How many pizzas were sold on Monday?

Type	Monday	Tuesday
Cheese	15	8
Pepperoni	6	9
Pineapple	2	11

23 pizzas

1

Type	Monday	Tuesday
Cheese	9	0
Pepperoni	6	10
Pineapple	5	6

_____ pizzas

4

Type	Monday	Tuesday
Cheese	22	18
Pepperoni	14	16
Pineapple	30	17

_____ pizzas

2

Type	Sunday	Monday
Cheese	15	9
Pepperoni	6	15
Pineapple	11	10

_____ pizzas

5

Type	Friday	Monday
Cheese	28	21
Pepperoni	16	17
Pineapple	5	15

_____ pizzas

3

Type	Monday	Friday
Cheese	20	12
Pepperoni	14	2
Pineapple	8	18

_____ pizzas

6

Type	Sunday	Monday
Cheese	19	15
Pepperoni	20	16
Pineapple	9	23

_____ pizzas

Today I scored _____ out of 6.

Week 1 — Day 3

Write in the missing number to complete the calculation.   4 × [10] = 40

1) 2 × ☐ = 10

2) ☐ ÷ 3 = 2

3) 10 × ☐ = 60

4) 28 ÷ ☐ = 4

5) ☐ ÷ 5 = 9

6) 3 × ☐ = 24

7) ☐ ÷ 4 = 12

8) 18 ÷ ☐ = 3

9) 4 × ☐ = 20

10) ☐ ÷ 12 = 5

11) ☐ × 11 = 33

12) ☐ × 6 = 24

13) 32 ÷ ☐ = 8

14) 9 × ☐ = 27

Today I scored ☐ out of 14.

Week 1 — Day 4

The person with more toy soldiers gives half of theirs to Katie. How many toy soldiers is Katie given?

Tim has 22 toy soldiers and Hans has 18 toy soldiers.

Katie gets **11** toy soldiers.

1) Tim has 8 toy soldiers and Hans has 12 toy soldiers.
Katie gets ☐ toy soldiers.

2) Tim has 20 toy soldiers and Hans has 16 toy soldiers.
Katie gets ☐ toy soldiers.

3) Tim has 18 toy soldiers and Hans has 8 toy soldiers.
Katie gets ☐ toy soldiers.

4) Tim has 24 toy soldiers and Hans has 22 toy soldiers.
Katie gets ☐ toy soldiers.

5) Tim has 26 toy soldiers and Hans has 30 toy soldiers.
Katie gets ☐ toy soldiers.

6) Tim has 50 toy soldiers and Hans has 40 toy soldiers.
Katie gets ☐ toy soldiers.

7) Tim has 32 toy soldiers and Hans has 24 toy soldiers.
Katie gets ☐ toy soldiers.

8) Tim has 80 toy soldiers and Hans has 88 toy soldiers.
Katie gets ☐ toy soldiers.

9) Tim has 28 toy soldiers and Hans has 36 toy soldiers.
Katie gets ☐ toy soldiers.

10) Tim has 58 toy soldiers and Hans has 54 toy soldiers.
Katie gets ☐ toy soldiers.

Today I scored ☐ out of 10.

Week 1 — Day 5

Write down the answer to the subtraction.

138 − 17 = 121

1) 345 − 30 =

2) 351 − 200 =

3) 63 − 30 =

4) 85 − 41 =

5) 54 − 44 =

6) 134 − 13 =

7) 92 − 61 =

8) 75 − 36 =

9) 616 − 9 =

10) 194 − 6 =

11) 536 − 80 =

12) 83 − 58 =

13) 244 − 92 =

14) 913 − 35 =

Today I scored ☐ out of 14.

Week 2 — Day 1

Fill in the boxes to complete the calculations.

− 9	807	+ 30
798		837

1 153: − 30 → ☐ ; + 600 → ☐

2 677: − 400 → ☐ ; + 20 → ☐

3 210: − 200 → ☐ ; + 7 → ☐

4 296: − 8 → ☐ ; + 300 → ☐

5 518: − 400 → ☐ ; + 6 → ☐

6 470: − 80 → ☐ ; + 9 → ☐

7 131: − 70 → ☐ ; + 9 → ☐

8 450: − 4 → ☐ ; + 90 → ☐

9 977: − 80 → ☐ ; + 8 → ☐

10 594: − 5 → ☐ ; + 30 → ☐

11 746: − 60 → ☐ ; + 7 → ☐

12 817: − 40 → ☐ ; + 5 → ☐

Today I scored ☐ out of 12.

Week 2 — Day 3

Write the three numbers in order from smallest to largest.

327, 273, 283

| 273 | 283 | 327 |

1) 545, 67, 429

6) 651, 811, 561

2) 408, 70, 37

7) 738, 747, 195

3) 124, 610, 179

8) 120, 102, 209

4) 735, 277, 728

9) 538, 358, 385

5) 129, 334, 127

10) 215, 251, 213

Today I scored ☐ out of 10.

Year 3 Mental Maths — Spring Term © CGP — Not to be photocopied

Week 2 — Day 4

How long will Sheila's supplies last?

Sheila has 10 pineapples and 14 coconuts. She eats 3 items of fruit every week.

8 weeks

1) Sheila has 25 oranges and 15 figs. She eats 10 items of fruit every week.

☐ weeks

2) Sheila has 9 bananas and 13 mangos. She eats 2 items of fruit every week.

☐ weeks

3) Sheila has 30 figs and 15 pineapples. She eats 5 items of fruit every week.

☐ weeks

4) Sheila has 12 coconuts and 16 bananas. She eats 4 items of fruit every week.

☐ weeks

5) Sheila has 18 mangos and 14 oranges. She eats 4 items of fruit every week.

☐ weeks

6) Sheila has 9 oranges and 18 coconuts. She eats 3 items of fruit every week.

☐ weeks

7) Sheila has 18 pineapples and 18 mangos. She eats 3 items of fruit every week.

☐ weeks

8) Sheila has 25 bananas and 19 figs. She eats 4 items of fruit every week.

☐ weeks

Today I scored ☐ out of 8.

Week 2 — Day 5

Write down the answer to the calculation.

424 + 28 = 452

1) 714 + 60 =

2) 924 − 500 =

3) 903 + 33 =

4) 761 − 51 =

5) 388 − 37 =

6) 302 + 19 =

7) 769 − 43 =

8) 459 + 4 =

9) 588 + 60 =

10) 301 − 5 =

11) 217 + 34 =

12) 421 + 94 =

13) 516 − 61 =

14) 342 − 56 =

Today I scored ☐ out of 14.

Year 3 Mental Maths — Spring Term

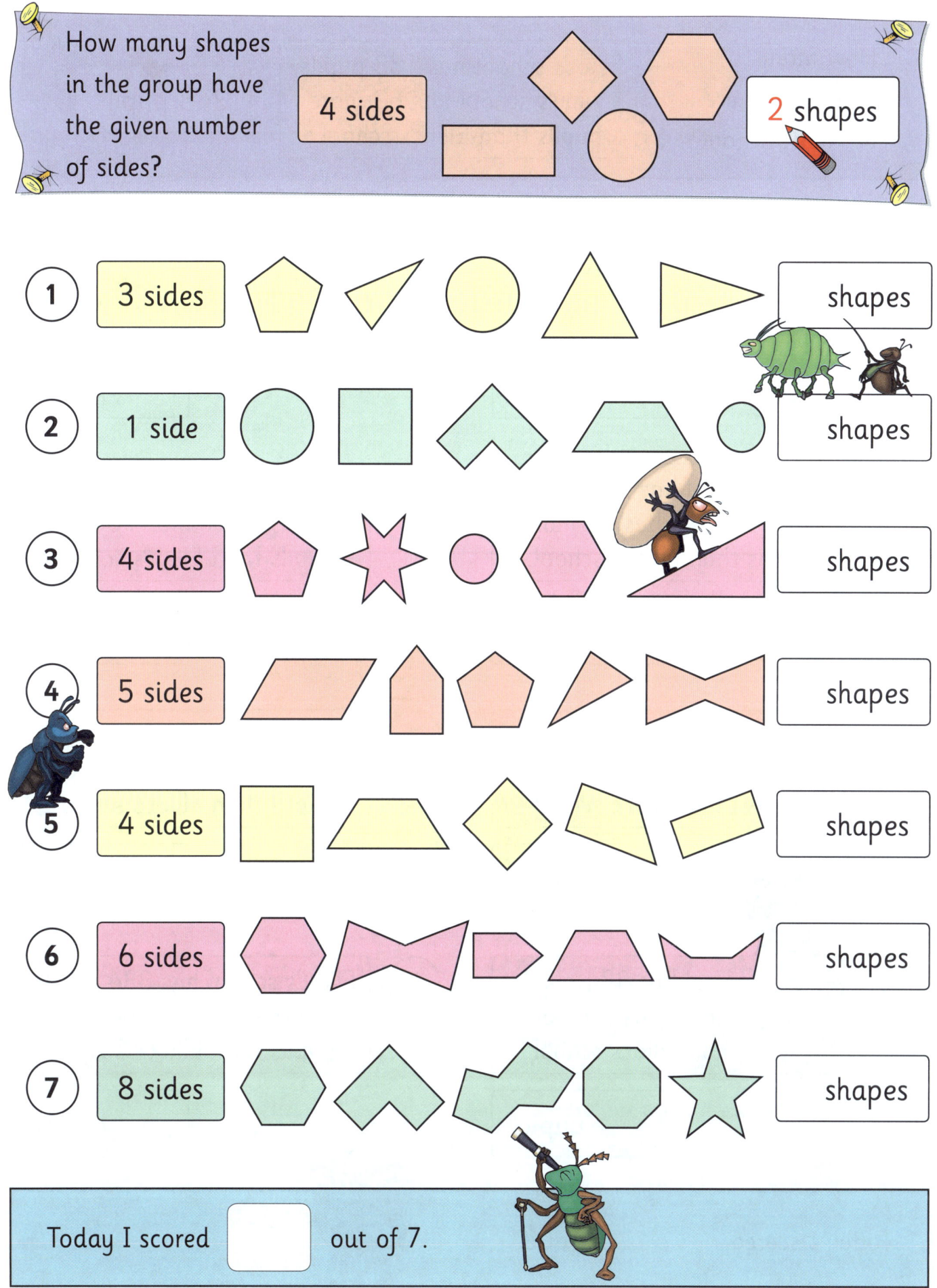

Week 3 — Day 2

How many pupils are there in Vijay's school?   Elliot's school has 188 pupils. Vijay's school has 60 more pupils than Elliot's school.   **248** pupils

1) Elliot's school has 164 pupils. Vijay's school has 20 more pupils than Elliot's school.

_____ pupils

2) Elliot's school has 267 pupils. Vijay's school has 30 more pupils than Elliot's school.

_____ pupils

3) Elliot's school has 180 pupils. Vijay's school has 20 more pupils than Elliot's school.

_____ pupils

4) Elliot's school has 384 pupils. Vijay's school has 50 more pupils than Elliot's school.

_____ pupils

5) Elliot's school has 582 pupils. Vijay's school has 30 more pupils than Elliot's school.

_____ pupils

6) Elliot's school has 439 pupils. Vijay's school has 70 more pupils than Elliot's school.

_____ pupils

7) Elliot's school has 693 pupils. Vijay's school has 40 more pupils than Elliot's school.

_____ pupils

8) Elliot's school has 334 pupils. Vijay's school has 90 more pupils than Elliot's school.

_____ pupils

Today I scored _____ out of 8.

Week 3 — Day 3

Make the smallest possible 3-digit number using the green cards, then follow the instruction on the yellow card.

| 7 | 3 | 6 | + 40 |

= 407

1) | 6 | 8 | 2 | + 30 | =

2) | 7 | 9 | 1 | − 100 | =

3) | 1 | 6 | 2 | + 60 | =

4) | 9 | 1 | 7 | + 400 | =

5) | 2 | 9 | 2 | − 20 | =

6) | 8 | 6 | 9 | − 300 | =

7) | 9 | 3 | 9 | + 50 | =

8) | 2 | 7 | 1 | − 40 | =

9) | 3 | 8 | 6 | + 80 | =

10) | 5 | 9 | 4 | − 70 | =

Today I scored [ ] out of 10.

Week 3 — Day 4

What is the difference between the numbers that the two arrows point to?

70

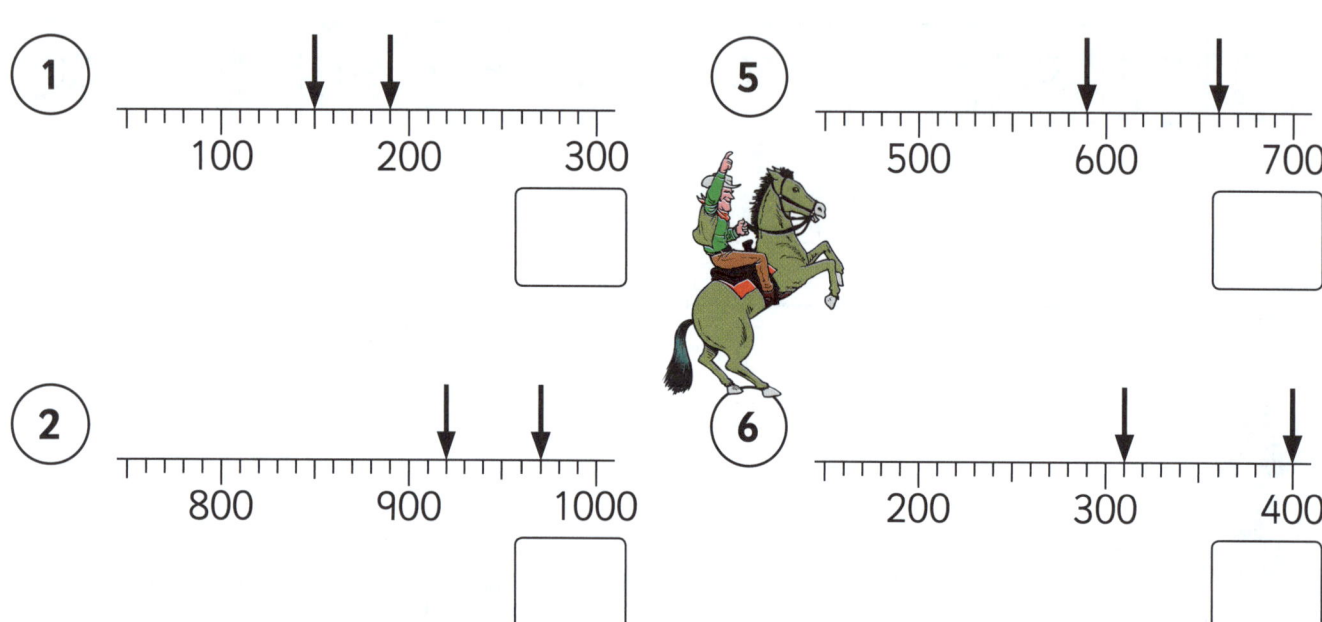

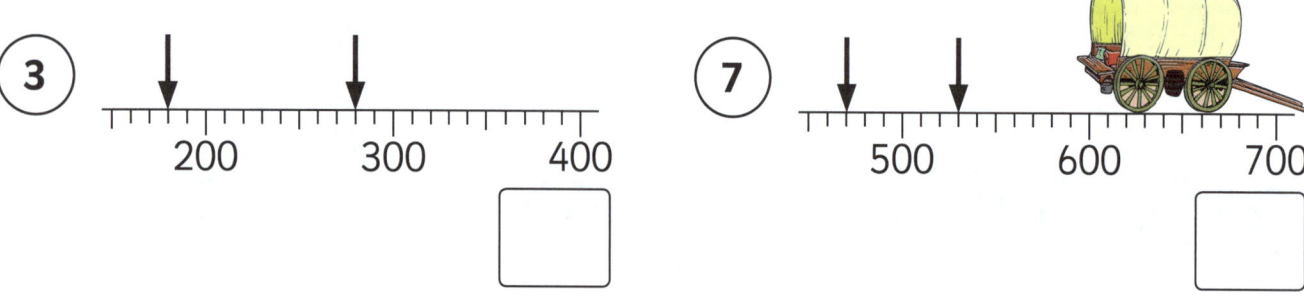

Today I scored ☐ out of 8.

Week 3 — Day 5

Jill, Karen and Lisa each think of a number. Use the information to fill in the missing numbers.

Jill's number is half of Karen's number. Lisa's number is three less than Jill's number.

Jill: 11   Karen: 22   Lisa: 8

1) Karen's number is three times Jill's number. Lisa's number is half of Karen's number.

Jill: 8   Karen: Lisa:

2) Jill's number is ten more than Lisa's number. Karen's number is four times Lisa's number.

Jill: Karen: Lisa: 11

3) Karen's number is eleven more than Lisa's number, and seven less than Jill's number.

Jill: Karen: Lisa: 9

4) Lisa's number is a quarter of Jill's number, and a third of Karen's number.

Jill: 36   Karen: Lisa:

5) Lisa's number is twice Jill's number. Karen's number is the difference between Lisa and Jill's numbers.

Jill: 30   Karen: Lisa:

6) Karen's number is eight less than Lisa's number. Jill's number is the sum of Karen and Lisa's numbers.

Jill: Karen: Lisa: 32

7) Jill's number is seven less than Karen's number. The three numbers add up to fifty.

Jill: Karen: 16   Lisa:

Today I scored [ ] out of 7.

Week 4 — Day 1

Write the lengths in order from the shortest to the longest.

| 32 m | 62 m | 16 m |
| 16 m | 32 m | 62 m |

1. 11 m   9 m   30 m
   ___ m   ___ m   ___ m

2. 13 m   97 m   58 m
   ___ m   ___ m   ___ m

3. 29 m   23 m   20 m
   ___ m   ___ m   ___ m

4. 54 m   56 m   45 m
   ___ m   ___ m   ___ m

5. 108 m   88 m   80 m
   ___ m   ___ m   ___ m

6. 132 m   146 m   222 m
   ___ m   ___ m   ___ m

7. 803 m   801 m   805 m
   ___ m   ___ m   ___ m

8. 375 m   377 m   357 m
   ___ m   ___ m   ___ m

9. 462 m   426 m   425 m
   ___ m   ___ m   ___ m

10. 356 m   536 m   365 m
    ___ m   ___ m   ___ m

Today I scored ___ out of 10.

Year 3 Mental Maths — Spring Term

Week 4 — Day 2

What is the total length of pipe?

3 pieces of pipe measuring 4 metres each. **12** m

1. 5 pieces of pipe measuring 2 metres each. ___ m
2. 6 pieces of pipe measuring 2 metres each. ___ m
3. 4 pieces of pipe measuring 5 metres each. ___ m
4. 10 pieces of pipe measuring 10 metres each. ___ m 
5. 9 pieces of pipe measuring 3 metres each. ___ m
6. 8 pieces of pipe measuring 5 metres each. ___ m
7. 12 pieces of pipe measuring 5 metres each. ___ m 
8. 10 pieces of pipe measuring 12 metres each. ___ m
9. 7 pieces of pipe measuring 4 metres each. ___ m
10. 3 pieces of pipe measuring 11 metres each. ___ m
11. 4 pieces of pipe measuring 8 metres each. ___ m
12. 4 pieces of pipe measuring 11 metres each. ___ m

Today I scored ___ out of 12.

Week 4 — Day 3

Complete the division.   30 ÷ 3 = 10

1) 12 ÷ 2 =
2) 20 ÷ 5 =
3) 90 ÷ 10 =
4) 22 ÷ 2 =
5) 120 ÷ 10 =
6) 40 ÷ 4 =
7) 45 ÷ 5 =
8) 24 ÷ 3 =
9) 28 ÷ 4 =
10) 18 ÷ 3 =
11) 60 ÷ 5 =
12) 36 ÷ 4 =
13) 33 ÷ 3 =
14) 48 ÷ 4 =

Today I scored ☐ out of 14.

Week 4 — Day 4

Complete the calculation.   50 mm + [30] mm = 80 mm

1) 70 mm + [   ] mm = 90 mm

2) 120 cm − [   ] cm = 80 cm

3) 200 mm − [   ] mm = 130 mm

4) [   ] m + 400 m = 820 m

5) [   ] m + 70 m = 350 m

6) [   ] cm − 247 cm = 70 cm

7) 205 cm + [   ] cm = 505 cm

8) 166 cm − [   ] cm = 116 cm

9) [   ] m − 181 m = 90 m

10) 564 cm − [   ] cm = 64 cm

11) 811 cm − [   ] cm = 761 cm

12) [   ] m + 479 m = 879 m

Today I scored [   ] out of 12.

Week 4 — Day 5

Calculate the total length in mm.

50 mm + 2 cm = 70 mm

1) 60 mm + 1 cm = ___ mm

2) 40 mm + 4 cm = ___ mm

3) 80 mm + 5 cm = ___ mm

4) 33 mm + 3 cm = ___ mm

5) 2 cm + 50 mm = ___ mm

6) 110 mm + 6 cm = ___ mm

7) 468 mm + 2 cm = ___ mm

8) 3 cm + 554 mm = ___ mm

9) 10 cm + 205 mm = ___ mm

10) 70 mm + 12 cm = ___ mm

11) 90 mm + 11 cm = ___ mm

12) 9 cm + 617 mm = ___ mm

Today I scored ___ out of 12.

Week 5 — Day 1

Complete the calculation. 2 × [2] = 4

1) ☐ × 3 = 12

2) 5 × ☐ = 10

3) ☐ × 5 = 20

4) 3 × ☐ = 9

5) ☐ × 3 = 27

6) 10 × ☐ = 120

7) ☐ × 5 = 45

8) ☐ × 4 = 36

9) ☐ × 3 = 36

10) 11 × ☐ = 22

11) 8 × ☐ = 24

12) 6 × ☐ = 30

13) 12 × ☐ = 48

14) 11 × ☐ = 110

Today I scored ☐ out of 14.

Week 5 — Day 2

Work out the perimeter of the shape. The sides of the shape have equal lengths.

4 cm ▢   **16 cm**

1) 6 cm ▢ ___ cm
2) 3 cm △ ___ cm
3) 7 cm ▢ ___ cm
4) 11 cm ▢ ___ cm
5) 3 cm ⬠ ___ cm
6) 9 cm △ ___ cm
7) 10 cm △ ___ cm
8) 9 cm ▢ ___ cm
9) 8 cm ⬠ ___ cm
10) 10 cm ⬠ ___ cm
11) 5 cm ⬡ ___ cm
12) 3 cm ⬛ ___ cm

Today I scored ___ out of 12.

Week 5 — Day 3

Complete the calculation.   23 + 52 = 75

1) 41 + 38 = ☐

2) 399 − 7 = ☐

3) 164 + 30 = ☐

4) 652 − 500 = ☐

5) 85 + 73 = ☐

6) 54 + ☐ = 77

7) ☐ − 55 = 93

8) ☐ + 300 = 623

9) ☐ − 600 = 84

10) 80 + ☐ = 123

11) ☐ + 90 = 147

12) ☐ − 80 = 451

13) 815 − ☐ = 115

14) 554 + ☐ = 594

Today I scored ☐ out of 14.

Week 5 — Day 4

James spends some of his money on a cake. How much money does James have left?

James has £15. He spends a third of it. He has £10 left.

1) James has £20. He spends half of it. He has £ ___ left.

2) James has £24. He spends half of it. He has £ ___ left.

3) James has £16. He spends a quarter of it. He has £ ___ left.

4) James has £12. He spends a third of it. He has £ ___ left.

5) James has £9. He spends a third of it. He has £ ___ left.

6) James has £32. He spends a quarter of it. He has £ ___ left.

7) James has £33. He spends a third of it. He has £ ___ left.

8) James has £48. He spends a quarter of it. He has £ ___ left.

9) James has £16. He spends three quarters of it. He has £ ___ left.

10) James has £28. He spends three quarters of it. He has £ ___ left.

Today I scored ___ out of 10.

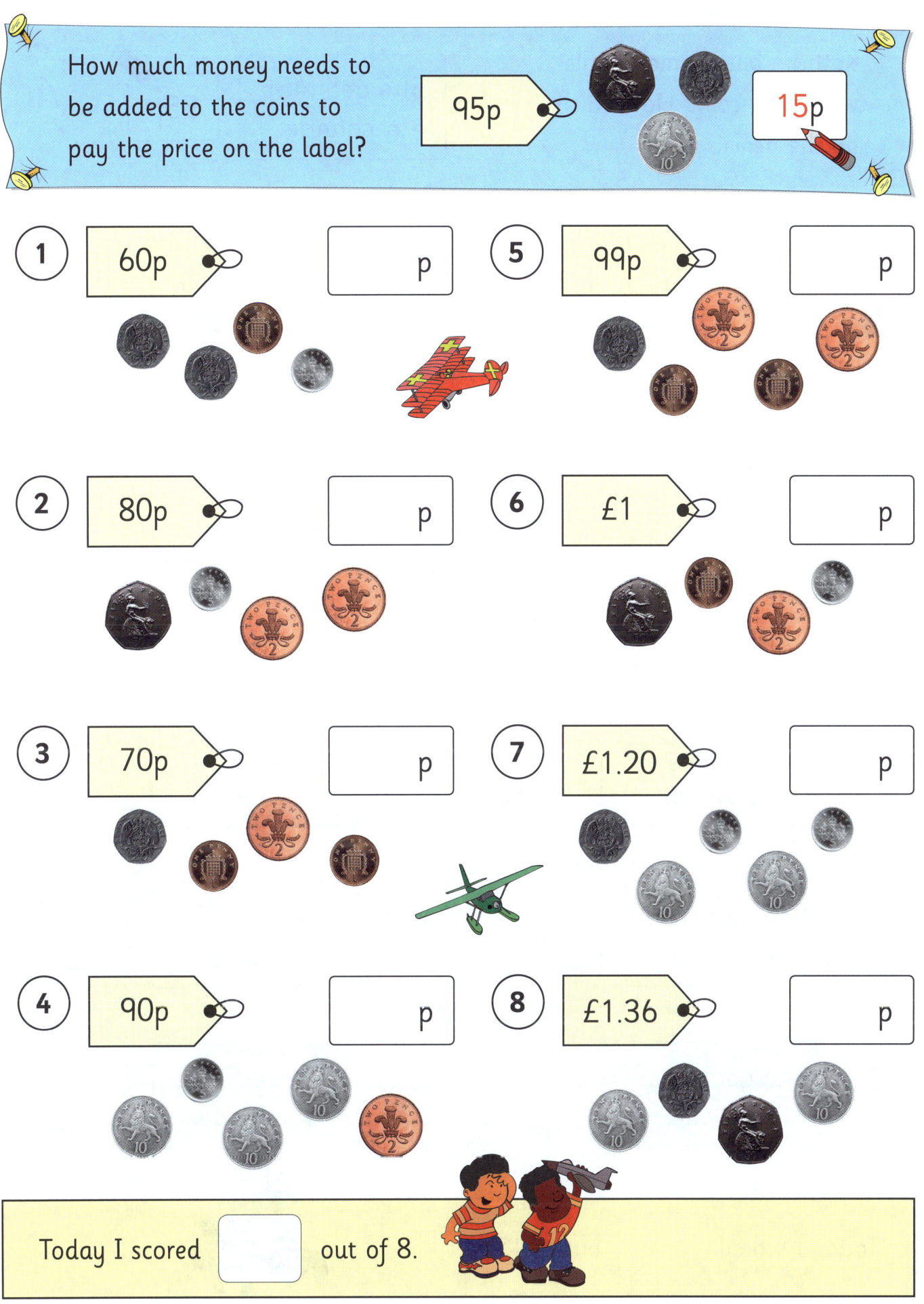

Week 6 — Day 1

Kathryn buys some pencils with a £1 coin. How much do the pencils cost?

She gets 45p in change. → 55p

#			#		
1	She gets 5p in change.	p	7	She gets 18p in change.	p
2	She gets 30p in change.	p	8	She gets 41p in change.	p
3	She gets 75p in change.	p	9	She gets 29p in change.	p
4	She gets 35p in change.	p	10	She gets 11p in change.	p
5	She gets 58p in change.	p	11	She gets 33p in change.	p
6	She gets 76p in change.	p	12	She gets 62p in change.	p

Today I scored ☐ out of 12.

Week 6 — Day 2

The pictogram shows how many people live in different villages. Complete the pictogram's key.

20 people live in Adbury.

Key: △ = 5 people

Village	People
Ramton	△△△
Adbury	△△△△

1

Village	People
Lunbridge	△△
Redhall	△△△

12 people live in Redhall.

Key: △ =   people

2

Village	People
Bowgreen	△△△
Kirbury	△△△△△

50 people live in Kirbury.

Key: △ =   people

3

Village	People
Henville	△△
Askford	△△△△

22 people live in Henville.

Key: △ =   people

4

Village	People
Lesford	△△△△
Vinehill	△△

28 people live in Lesford.

Key: △ =   people

5

Village	People
Olworth	△△△
Kenhill	△

27 people live in Olworth.

Key: △ =   people

6

Village	People
Strandon	△△
Marlton	△△△△△

35 people live in Marlton.

Key: △ =   people

Today I scored ☐ out of 6.

Week 6 — Day 3

The pictogram shows how many missions three astronauts have flown. How many more missions has Natalya flown than Wei?

David	🚀🚀
Wei	🚀
Natalya	🚀🚀🚀🚀

Key: 🚀 = 5 missions

15 missions

①

Key: 🚀 = 10 missions   _____ missions

②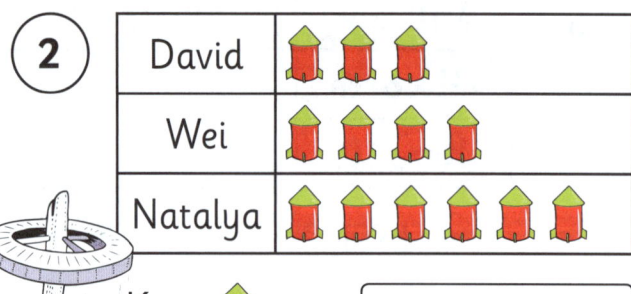

Key: 🚀 = 5 missions   _____ missions

③

Key: 🚀 = 4 missions   _____ missions

④

Key: 🚀 = 8 missions   _____ missions

⑤

Key: 🚀 = 6 missions   _____ missions

⑥

Key: 🚀 = 12 missions   _____ missions

Today I scored ☐ out of 6.

Week 6 — Day 4

Lance thinks of a number. He adds seven to the number, and then doubles it to get a new number. What is Lance's new number?

Lance's number: 24
New number: 62

1) Lance's number: 5
   New number:

2) Lance's number: 13
   New number:

3) Lance's number: 7
   New number:

4) Lance's number: 16
   New number:

5) Lance's number: 21
   New number:

6) Lance's number: 67
   New number:

7) Lance's number: 45
   New number:

8) Lance's number: 56
   New number:

9) Lance's number: 61
   New number:

10) Lance's number: 89
    New number:

Today I scored ☐ out of 10.

Week 6 — Day 5

Use the information to complete the pictogram showing how many pets Amelia's classmates own.

Cats	◯◯
Dogs	○○○○
Rabbits	◯

Key: ◯ = 5 animals

The number of dogs is ten more than the number of cats.

1

Horses	◯
Snakes	◯◯
Dogs	

Key: ◯ = 5 animals

The number of dogs is fifteen more than the number of horses.

2

Dogs	◯◯◯◯
Hens	
Cats	◯◯

Key: ◯ = 3 animals

The number of hens is nine more than the number of cats.

3

Cats	◯◯
Lizards	
Birds	◯◯◯◖

Key: ◯ = 4 animals

The number of lizards is eight less than the number of birds.

4

Rabbits	
Dogs	◯◖
Mice	◯◯◖

Key: ◯ = 8 animals

The number of rabbits is the number of dogs plus the number of mice.

5

Cats	◯◯
Horses	◯◖
Dogs	

Key: ◯ = 6 animals

The number of cats is nine less than the number of dogs.

Today I scored ☐ out of 5.

Week 7 — Day 1

Write < or > in the box.   45 kg > 60 g

1. 56 kg ☐ 64 kg
2. 99 g ☐ 113 g
3. 78 g ☐ 87 g
4. 243 kg ☐ 195 kg
5. 544 g ☐ 465 g
6. 808 kg ☐ 880 kg
7. 40 kg ☐ 94 g
8. 940 g ☐ 904 g
9. 341 g ☐ 314 g
10. 84 g ☐ 21 kg
11. 1 kg ☐ 100 g
12. 147 g ☐ 174 g

Today I scored ☐ out of 12.

Week 7 — Day 2

Write down the value of the given digit in the number.

Give the value of the 3 in 328. → 300

1. Give the value of the 6 in 506.
2. Give the value of the 7 in 670.
3. Give the value of the 1 in 914.
4. Give the value of the 4 in 462.
5. Give the value of the 2 in 235.
6. Give the value of the 8 in 78.
7. Give the value of the 5 in 654.
8. Give the value of the 3 in 309.
9. Give the value of the 5 in 751.
10. Give the value of the 9 in 529.
11. Give the value of the 4 in 400.
12. Give the value of the 7 in 760.
13. Give the value of the 6 in 163.
14. Give the value of the 3 in 903.

Today I scored [ ] out of 14.

Year 3 Mental Maths — Spring Term

Week 7 — Day 3

Tick the box to show whether the sentence is true or false.

95 + 52 is greater than 165.
☐ True   ✓ False

1) 31 + 33 is greater than 60.
☐ True   ☐ False

2) 24 + 42 is greater than 86.
☐ True   ☐ False

3) 55 + 23 is less than 80.
☐ True   ☐ False

4) 47 + 33 is greater than 77.
☐ True   ☐ False

5) 67 + 23 is greater than 91.
☐ True   ☐ False

6) 39 + 38 is less than 76.
☐ True   ☐ False

7) 80 + 62 is greater than 150.
☐ True   ☐ False

8) 85 + 72 is less than 166.
☐ True   ☐ False

9) 61 + 69 is greater than 123.
☐ True   ☐ False

10) 74 + 67 is greater than 142.
☐ True   ☐ False

11) 95 + 66 is less than 154.
☐ True   ☐ False

12) 95 + 95 is greater than 180.
☐ True   ☐ False

Today I scored ☐ out of 12.

Week 7 — Day 4

How much more flour does Max need for the recipe?

Recipe: 200 g

Max needs 40 g more.

1)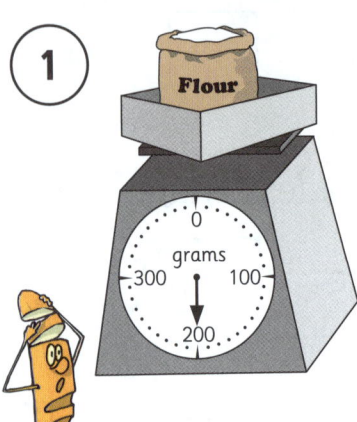

Recipe: 300 g

Max needs ☐ g more.

2)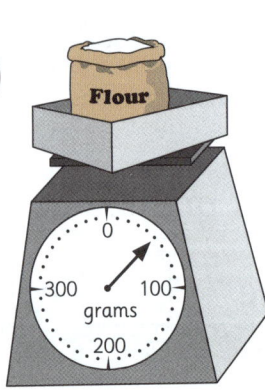

Recipe: 100 g

Max needs ☐ g more.

3)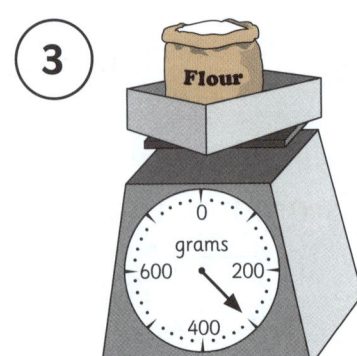

Recipe: 450 g

Max needs ☐ g more.

4)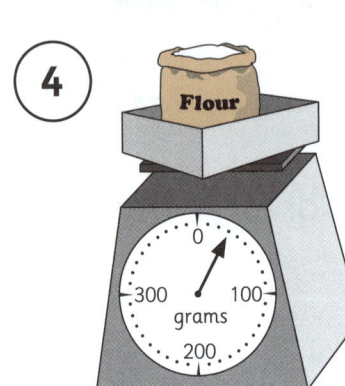

Recipe: 240 g

Max needs ☐ g more.

5)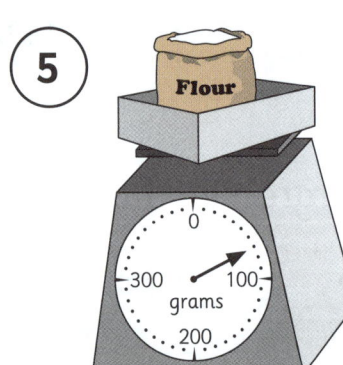

Recipe: 350 g

Max needs ☐ g more.

6)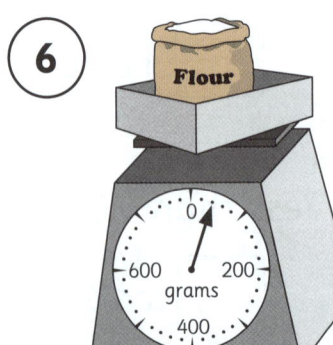

Recipe: 300 g

Max needs ☐ g more.

Today I scored ☐ out of 6.

Week 7 — Day 5

Start with the number in the yellow box and follow the instructions to work out the final number.

12 → ×10 → ÷2 → +10 → 70

1) 2 → ×8 → +2 → ÷2 → ☐

2) 5 → ×4 → ÷2 → +16 → ☐

3) 40 → ÷4 → ×3 → −5 → ☐

4) 6 → ×5 → ÷10 → +33 → ☐

5) 62 → −29 → ÷11 → ×5 → ☐

6) 75 → −69 → ×4 → ÷2 → ☐

7) 60 → ÷5 → ×3 → +61 → ☐

8) 90 → ÷10 → ×5 → +38 → ☐

Today I scored ☐ out of 8.

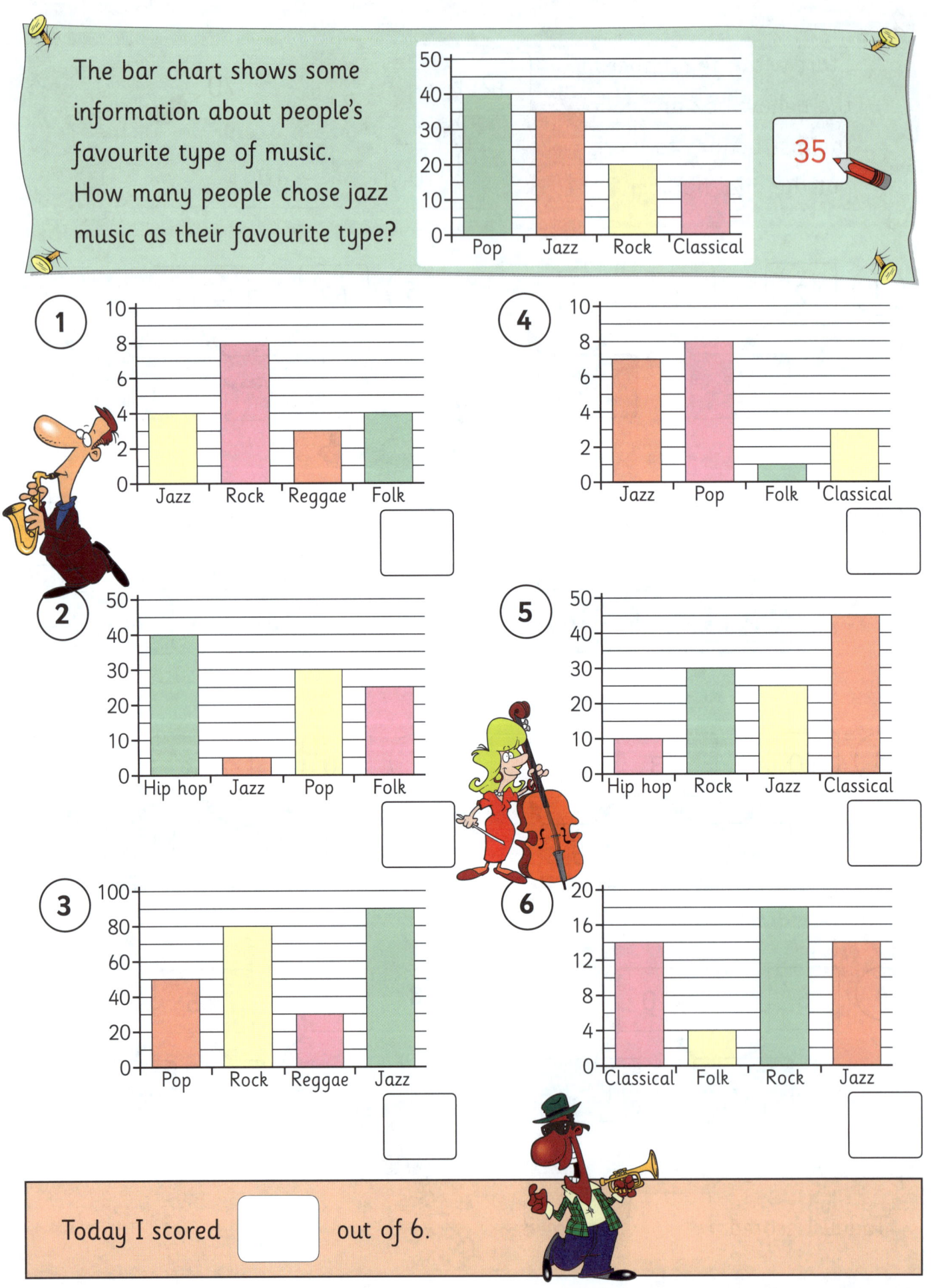

Week 8 — Day 2

Colin the camel is 200 cm long. How much longer is he than the animal shown?

Example: 186 cm

1. ____ cm
2. ____ cm
3. ____ cm
4. ____ cm
5. ____ cm
6. ____ cm
7. ____ cm
8. ____ cm

Today I scored ____ out of 8.

Week 8 — Day 3

The bar chart shows how many books three friends read in one year. Use the bar chart to answer the question.

(Bar chart: Rachel ≈ 9, Stef ≈ 12, Tom ≈ 21)

How many more books than Rachel did Tom read?

12

1. (Bar chart: Peter ≈ 23, Quinn ≈ 9, Rami ≈ 16)

How many more books than Quinn did Peter read? ☐

2. (Bar chart: Alana ≈ 38, Beth ≈ 18, Chris ≈ 12)

How many fewer books than Alana did Chris read? ☐

3. (Bar chart: Ed ≈ 14, Frank ≈ 11, Grace ≈ 6)

How many books did the three friends read in total? ☐

4. (Bar chart: Iona ≈ 28, Jo ≈ 40, Keith ≈ 22)

How many more books than Keith did Jo read? ☐

5. (Bar chart: Holly ≈ 24, Ian ≈ 40, Jamal ≈ 15)

How many books did the three friends read in total? ☐

6. (Bar chart: Levi ≈ 16, Maeve ≈ 18, Nadira ≈ 44)

How many more books than Levi and Maeve did Nadira read? ☐

Today I scored ☐ out of 6.

Week 8 — Day 4

Rearrange the number cards so the calculation gives the largest possible answer.

1 7 3 + 4 7

731 + 74 = 805

1) 1 3 6 + 8 2   __ + __ = __

2) 8 0 5 + 4 5   __ + __ = __

3) 7 4 5 + 6 0   __ + __ = __

4) 2 9 2 + 5 7   __ + __ = __

5) 1 8 8 + 3 9   __ + __ = __

6) 2 7 0 + 8 9   __ + __ = __

7) 7 7 5 + 3 5   __ + __ = __

8) 6 8 7 + 9 4   __ + __ = __

Today I scored ☐ out of 8.

Week 8 — Day 5

How many pupils play both rounders and baseball?

Amy's class has 32 rounders and baseball players. 18 pupils play rounders and 20 pupils play baseball.

6 pupils

1. Rich's class has 20 rounders and baseball players. 15 pupils play rounders and 13 pupils play baseball.

   ____ pupils

2. Dani's class has 31 rounders and baseball players. 22 pupils play rounders and 19 pupils play baseball.

   ____ pupils

3. Shreyus' year has 60 rounders and baseball players. 40 pupils play rounders and 37 pupils play baseball.

   ____ pupils

4. Greg's class has 28 rounders and baseball players. 21 pupils play rounders and 21 pupils play baseball.

   ____ pupils

5. Gina's class has 27 rounders and baseball players. 24 pupils play rounders and 19 pupils play baseball.

   ____ pupils

6. Simon's year has 55 rounders and baseball players. 38 pupils play rounders and 42 pupils play baseball.

   ____ pupils

7. Mary's class has 39 rounders and baseball players. 28 pupils play rounders and 27 pupils play baseball.

   ____ pupils

8. Nina's year has 89 rounders and baseball players. 63 pupils play rounders and 38 pupils play baseball.

   ____ pupils

Today I scored ____ out of 8.

Week 9 — Day 1

Complete the division. 36 ÷ 3 = 12

1) 20 ÷ 2 =
2) 80 ÷ 10 =
3) 16 ÷ 4 =
4) 35 ÷ 5 =
5) 32 ÷ 4 =
6) 21 ÷ 3 =
7) 55 ÷ 5 =
8) 27 ÷ 3 =
9) 52 ÷ 4 =
10) 30 ÷ 2 =
11) 200 ÷ 10 =
12) 44 ÷ 2 =
13) 60 ÷ 3 =
14) 56 ÷ 2 =

Today I scored ☐ out of 14.

Week 9 — Day 2

How many people like the food James asks them about?

James asks 20 people if they like bananas. $\frac{1}{5}$ of them say yes.

4 people like bananas.

1 James asks 18 people if they like sweetcorn. $\frac{1}{2}$ of them say yes.

☐ people like sweetcorn.

2 James asks 35 people if they like spinach. $\frac{1}{5}$ of them say yes.

☐ people like spinach.

3 James asks 60 people if they like cabbage. $\frac{1}{10}$ of them say yes.

☐ people like cabbage.

4 James asks 44 people if they like kiwi fruit. $\frac{1}{4}$ of them say yes.

☐ people like kiwi fruit.

5 James asks 24 people if they like carrots. $\frac{1}{3}$ of them say yes.

☐ people like carrots.

6 James asks 96 people if they like beetroot. $\frac{1}{8}$ of them say yes.

☐ people like beetroot.

7 James asks 36 people if they like mushrooms. $\frac{1}{4}$ of them say yes.

☐ people like mushrooms.

8 James asks 56 people if they like sprouts. $\frac{1}{8}$ of them say yes.

☐ people like sprouts.

Today I scored ☐ out of 8.

Week 9 — Day 3

How much did the person spend?

Ali bought 20 mugs. Mugs cost £3 each. £60

1. Jon bought 9 pens. Pens cost £2 each. £

2. Sunny bought 12 mugs. Mugs cost £3 each. £

3. Gary bought 14 hats. Hats cost £10 each. £

4. Mo bought 20 cards. Cards cost £5 each. £

5. Freya bought 14 cards. Cards cost £5 each. £

6. Ruvi bought 30 mugs. Mugs cost £3 each. £

7. Eliza bought 25 bottles. Bottles cost £4 each. £

8. Anna bought 33 pens. Pens cost £2 each. £

9. Zak bought 15 mugs. Mugs cost £3 each. £

10. Kate bought 17 bottles. Bottles cost £4 each. £

Today I scored ☐ out of 10.

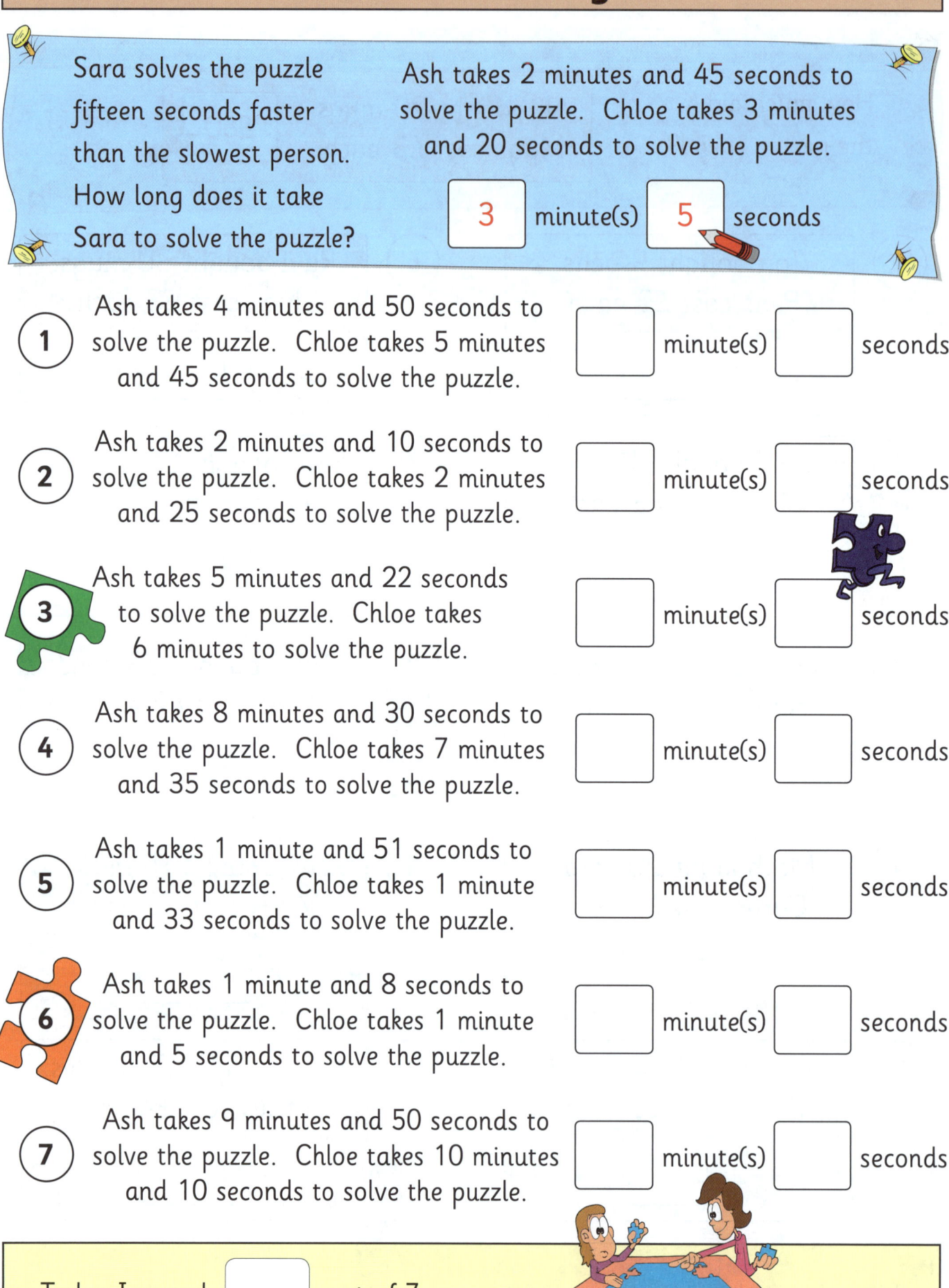

Week 9 — Day 5

Daisy the dragon flies the same distance every day. Answer the question about the total distance Daisy flies.

Daisy flies 36 km in 3 days. How far does she fly in 10 days?

120 km

1. Daisy flies 12 km in 2 days. How far does she fly in 10 days? ___ km

2. Daisy flies 25 km in 5 days. How far does she fly in 12 days? ___ km

3. Daisy flies 40 km in 4 days. How far does she fly in 21 days? ___ km

4. Daisy flies 20 km in 5 days. How far does she fly in 30 days? ___ km

5. Daisy flies 15 km in 3 days. How far does she fly in 15 days? ___ km

6. Daisy flies 16 km in 4 days. How far does she fly in 13 days? ___ km

7. Daisy flies 22 km in 11 days. How far does she fly in 36 days? ___ km

Today I scored ___ out of 7.

Week 10 — Day 1

Write in the missing number to complete the calculation.

$32 \div 8 = \boxed{4}$

1) $2 \times 8 = \boxed{}$

2) $\boxed{} \div 4 = 6$

3) $5 \times \boxed{} = 40$

4) $3 \times 8 = \boxed{}$

5) $\boxed{} \div 4 = 4$

6) $80 \div \boxed{} = 10$

7) $\boxed{} \div 3 = 12$

8) $7 \times 8 = \boxed{}$

9) $\boxed{} \div 6 = 8$

10) $\boxed{} \times 5 = 60$

11) $64 \div 8 = \boxed{}$

12) $\boxed{} \times 8 = 72$

13) $8 \times \boxed{} = 96$

14) $88 \div \boxed{} = 8$

Today I scored ☐ out of 14.

Week 10 — Day 2

Fill in the boxes so that they show a sequence of numbers counting up in steps of eight.

| 8 | 16 | 24 | 32 |

1. | 0 | | | |

2. | | | | 40 |

3. | 40 | | | |

4. | 64 | | | |

5. | | | | 32 |

6. | | 32 | | |

7. | | | 64 | |

8. | 56 | | | |

9. | | | | 56 |

10. | | | 88 | |

Today I scored [ ] out of 10.

Week 10 — Day 3

How many people are in the shop at the end of the hour?

There are 24 people in a shop. In the next hour, 20 people enter the shop and 27 people leave.

17 people

1. There are 50 people in a shop. In the next hour, 45 people enter the shop and 15 people leave.

   ☐ people

2. There are 26 people in a shop. In the next hour, 14 people enter the shop and 20 people leave.

   ☐ people

3. There are 70 people in a shop. In the next hour, 16 people enter the shop and 25 people leave.

   ☐ people

4. There are 36 people in a shop. In the next hour, 25 people enter the shop and 13 people leave.

   ☐ people

5. There are 18 people in a shop. In the next hour, 30 people enter the shop and 19 people leave.

   ☐ people

6. There are 34 people in a shop. In the next hour, 26 people enter the shop and 14 people leave.

   ☐ people

7. There are 87 people in a shop. In the next hour, 29 people enter the shop and 14 people leave.

   ☐ people

8. There are 67 people in a shop. In the next hour, 56 people enter the shop and 18 people leave.

   ☐ people

Today I scored ☐ out of 8.

Week 10 — Day 4

Follow the instructions in the boxes to work out the final answer.

120 → ÷ 10 → × 8 → 96

1) 6 → + 5 → × 8 → − 14 → ☐

2) 77 → − 17 → ÷ 10 → × 8 → ☐

3) 23 → − 15 → × 4 → + 28 → ☐

4) 250 → ÷ 10 → + 7 → ÷ 8 → ☐

5) 42 → − 39 → × 8 → × 10 → ☐

6) 10 → × 8 → + 70 → ÷ 10 → ☐

7) 25 → − 9 → × 4 → ÷ 8 → ☐

8) 60 → − 48 → × 8 → + 35 → ☐

Today I scored ☐ out of 8.

Week 10 — Day 5

How much money do Aaman and Bianca end up with?

Aaman has £1.20 and Bianca has £2.45. Aaman gives 50p to Bianca.

Aaman: £0.70   Bianca: £2.95

1) Aaman has £5.30 and Bianca has £2.95. Aaman gives £5 to Bianca.

Aaman: £ ____   Bianca: £ ____

2) Aaman has £4.50 and Bianca has £2.80. Bianca gives 70p to Aaman.

Aaman: £ ____   Bianca: £ ____

3) Aaman has £5.80 and Bianca has £6.70. Bianca gives 65p to Aaman.

Aaman: £ ____   Bianca: £ ____

4) Aaman has £4.50 and Bianca has £2.75. Aaman gives £1.50 to Bianca.

Aaman: £ ____   Bianca: £ ____

5) Aaman has £1.60 and Bianca has £7.95. Bianca gives £2.50 to Aaman.

Aaman: £ ____   Bianca: £ ____

6) Aaman has £7.20 and Bianca has £6.85. Aaman gives £2.50 to Bianca.

Aaman: £ ____   Bianca: £ ____

Today I scored ____ out of 6.

Week 11 — Day 1

Write the three numbers in order from lowest to highest.

153, 252, 135

135 **153** **252**

1) 511, 518, 185

2) 950, 592, 959

3) 201, 271, 210

4) 874, 418, 478

5) 634, 643, 622

6) 331, 133, 131

7) 179, 719, 197

8) 886, 864, 846

9) 703, 307, 730

10) 118, 811, 181

11) 628, 268, 286

12) 512, 522, 521

Today I scored ☐ out of 12.

Week 11 — Day 2

Fill in the boxes to complete the calculations.

− 70 ← 616 → + 70
546 , 686

1) − 5 ← 116 → + 5
2) − 300 ← 391 → + 300
3) − 200 ← 683 → + 200
4) − 70 ← 412 → + 70
5) − 8 ← 896 → + 8
6) − 60 ← 543 → + 60
7) − 9 ← 227 → + 9
8) − 80 ← 521 → + 80
9) − 12 ← 955 → + 12
10) − 31 ← 258 → + 31
11) − 25 ← 180 → + 25
12) − 28 ← 324 → + 28

Today I scored ☐ out of 12.

Week 11 — Day 3

Complete the fraction in the box to show what fraction of the sheep are white.

$\dfrac{1}{3}$

1. $\dfrac{1}{6}$

2. $\dfrac{1}{5}$

3. $\dfrac{1}{7}$

4. $\dfrac{1}{9}$

5. $\dfrac{1}{8}$

6. $\dfrac{1}{5}$

7. $\dfrac{1}{3}$

8. $\dfrac{1}{4}$

9. $\dfrac{1}{10}$

10. $\dfrac{1}{4}$

Today I scored ☐ out of 10.

Week 11 — Day 4

Write in the missing number to complete the sentence.

30 is $\frac{1}{2}$ of 60

1) 5 is $\frac{1}{2}$ of ☐

2) 6 is $\frac{1}{10}$ of ☐

3) 6 is $\frac{1}{5}$ of ☐

4) 11 is $\frac{1}{3}$ of ☐

5) 9 is $\frac{1}{5}$ of ☐

6) 8 is $\frac{1}{4}$ of ☐

7) 20 is $\frac{1}{3}$ of ☐

8) 25 is $\frac{1}{2}$ of ☐

9) 16 is $\frac{1}{4}$ of ☐

10) 12 is $\frac{2}{3}$ of ☐

11) 20 is $\frac{2}{5}$ of ☐

12) 36 is $\frac{3}{4}$ of ☐

Today I scored ☐ out of 12.

Week 11 — Day 5

The table shows how many pupils at a school study different subjects. Use the fact to complete the table.

	Boys	Girls
Art	89	64
Drama	42	96
Music	66	41

55 more girls study drama than music.

1

	Boys	Girls
Art	26	37
Drama	13	21
Music		51

40 more boys study music than art.

2

	Boys	Girls
Art		29
Drama	37	45
Music	22	38

There are 35 more boys than girls studying art.

3

	Boys	Girls
Art	37	53
Drama	65	
Music	80	49

100 pupils study drama.

4

	Boys	Girls
Art	17	
Drama	55	
Music	22	15

20 more boys than girls study drama. 5 fewer girls study art than drama.

5

	Boys	Girls
Art		
Drama	14	18
Music	56	66

22 more boys study music than art. 50 pupils in total study art.

6

	Boys	Girls
Art	39	
Drama	11	26
Music	55	42

The number of girls studying art is 15 more than the number of pupils studying drama.

Today I scored ☐ out of 6.

Week 12 — Day 1

The bottles of juice are shared between ten friends. Write the fraction of a bottle that each person gets, and then draw an arrow to show the fraction's position on the number line.

1. [5 yellow bottles] ☐

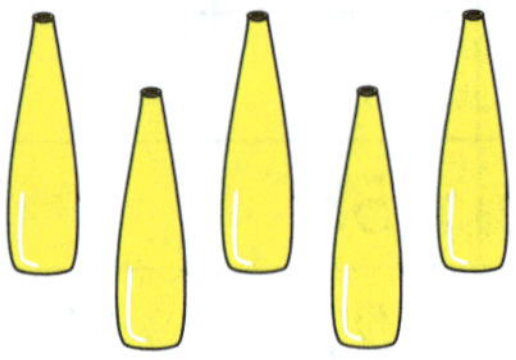

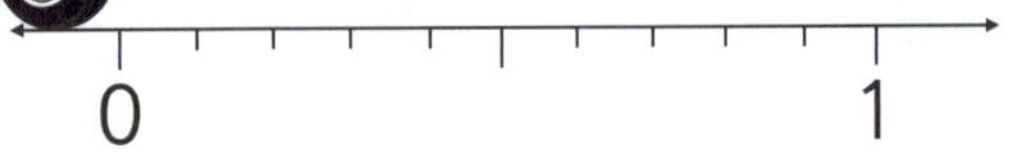

2. [4 red bottles] ☐

3. [6 dark bottles] ☐

4. [8 red bottles] ☐

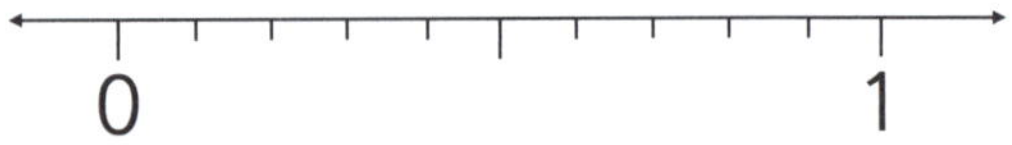

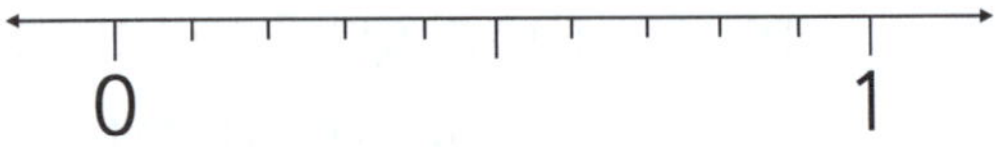

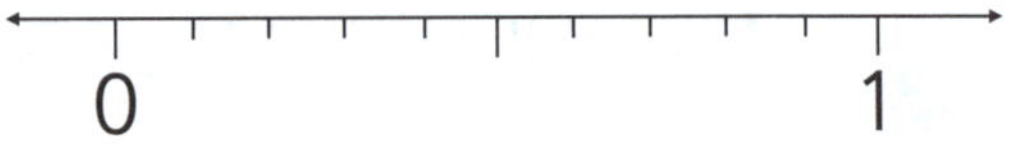

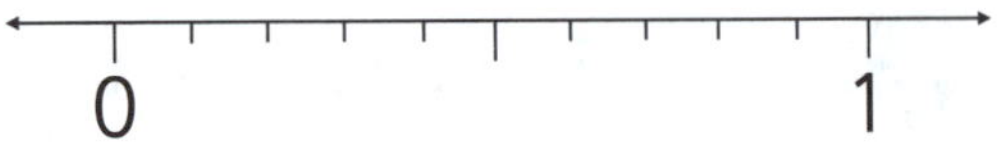

5. [3 orange bottles] ☐

6. [7 yellow bottles] ☐

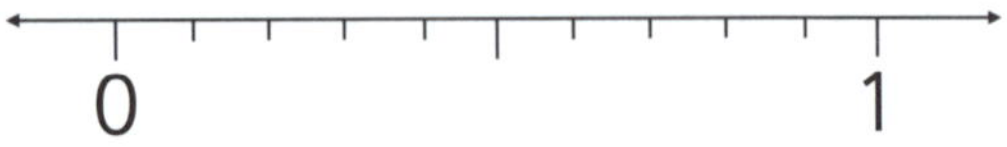

Today I scored ☐ out of 6.

Week 12 — Day 2

Complete the division. 33 ÷ 3 = 11

1) 16 ÷ 2 =
2) 70 ÷ 10 =
3) 45 ÷ 5 =
4) 80 ÷ 8 =
5) 20 ÷ 4 =
6) 18 ÷ 3 =
7) 24 ÷ 3 =
8) 32 ÷ 8 =
9) 36 ÷ 4 =
10) 64 ÷ 8 =
11) 56 ÷ 8 =
12) 48 ÷ 4 =
13) 48 ÷ 2 =
14) 96 ÷ 8 =

Today I scored ☐ out of 14.

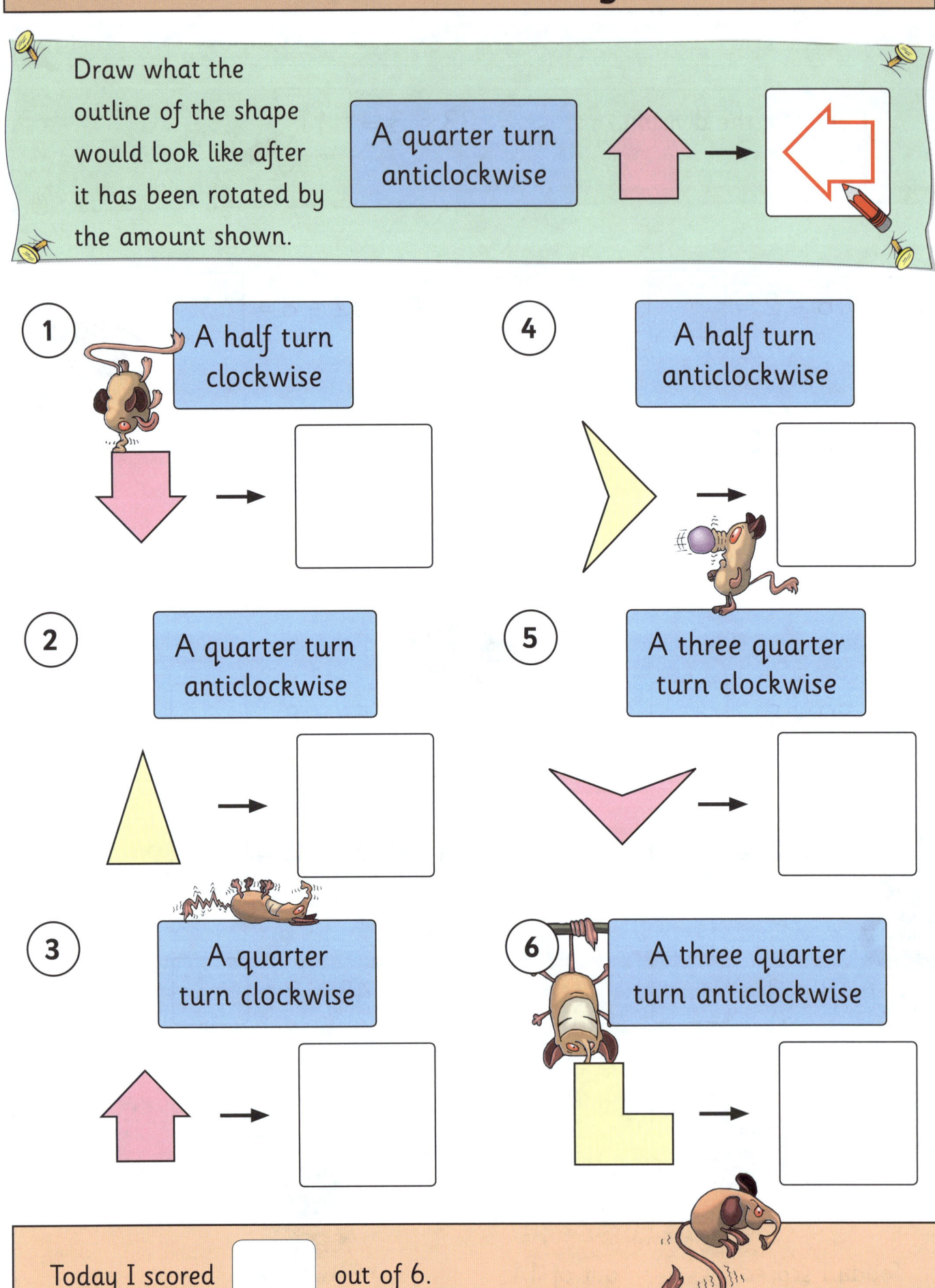

Week 12 — Day 4

How many days will it take for the person to reach their goal?

Ali cycles 8 km a day. His goal is to cycle 50 km. **7** days

1) Zara cycles 5 km a day. Her goal is to cycle 39 km. ___ days

2) Abdul cycles 10 km a day. His goal is to cycle 85 km. ___ days

3) Holly cycles 2 km a day. Her goal is to cycle 21 km. ___ days

4) Clem cycles 4 km a day. His goal is to cycle 30 km. ___ days

5) Arthur cycles 10 km a day. His goal is to cycle 111 km. ___ days

6) Deepa cycles 3 km a day. Her goal is to cycle 25 km. ___ days

7) Wanda cycles 4 km a day. Her goal is to cycle 25 km. ___ days

8) Lee cycles 8 km a day. His goal is to cycle 42 km. ___ days

9) Eva cycles 3 km a day. Her goal is to cycle 35 km. ___ days

10) Agnes cycles 8 km a day. Her goal is to cycle 70 km. ___ days

Today I scored ___ out of 10.

Week 12 — Day 5

Write the fraction of the group of shapes that each type of shape makes up.

Striped shapes: $\frac{3}{5}$

Squares: $\frac{2}{5}$

1. Striped shapes:

   Striped circles:

2. Circles:

   Spotted shapes:

3. Four-sided shapes:

   Striped triangles:

4. Triangles:

   Spotted shapes:

Today I scored ☐ out of 4.

Answers

Week 1 — Day 1
1. 200, 300, 400, 500, **600**, **700**
2. **500**, **600**, 700, 800, 900, 1000
3. 100, **200**, 300, **400**, 500, 600
4. **500**, 400, **300**, 200, 100, 0
5. 900, 800, **700**, **600**, 500, 400
6. 400, 500, 600, **700**, **800**, 900
7. 1100, 1000, 900, 800, **700**, **600**
8. 700, 800, 900, **1000**, 1100, **1200**

Week 1 — Day 2
1. 20 pizzas
2. 34 pizzas
3. 42 pizzas
4. 66 pizzas
5. 53 pizzas
6. 54 pizzas

Week 1 — Day 3
1. 5
2. 6
3. 6
4. 7
5. 45
6. 8
7. 48
8. 6
9. 5
10. 60
11. 3
12. 4
13. 4
14. 3

Week 1 — Day 4
1. 6
2. 10
3. 9
4. 12
5. 15
6. 25
7. 16
8. 44
9. 18
10. 29

Week 1 — Day 5
1. 315
2. 151
3. 33
4. 44
5. 10
6. 121
7. 31
8. 39
9. 607
10. 188
11. 456
12. 25
13. 152
14. 878

Week 2 — Day 1
1. 123, 753
2. 277, 697
3. 10, 217
4. 288, 596
5. 118, 524
6. 390, 479
7. 61, 140
8. 446, 540
9. 897, 985
10. 589, 624
11. 686, 753
12. 777, 822

Week 2 — Day 2
1. 3:30
2. 1:55
3. 10:20
4. 2:38
5. 11:13
6. 4:06
7. 6:54
8. 7:36
9. 5:29
10. 9:43

Week 2 — Day 3
1. 67, 429, 545
2. 37, 70, 408
3. 124, 179, 610
4. 277, 728, 735
5. 127, 129, 334
6. 561, 651, 811
7. 195, 738, 747
8. 102, 120, 209
9. 358, 385, 538
10. 213, 215, 251

Week 2 — Day 4
1. 4 weeks
2. 11 weeks
3. 9 weeks
4. 7 weeks
5. 8 weeks
6. 9 weeks
7. 12 weeks
8. 11 weeks

Week 2 — Day 5
1. 774
2. 424
3. 936
4. 710
5. 351
6. 321
7. 726
8. 463
9. 648
10. 296
11. 251
12. 515
13. 455
14. 286

Week 3 — Day 1
1. 3 shapes
2. 2 shapes
3. 0 shapes
4. 2 shapes
5. 5 shapes
6. 3 shapes
7. 2 shapes

Week 3 — Day 2
1. 184 pupils
2. 297 pupils
3. 200 pupils
4. 434 pupils
5. 612 pupils
6. 509 pupils
7. 733 pupils
8. 424 pupils

Week 3 — Day 3
1. 298
2. 79
3. 186
4. 579
5. 209
6. 389
7. 449
8. 87
9. 448
10. 389

Week 3 — Day 4
1. 40
2. 50
3. 100
4. 60
5. 70
6. 90
7. 60
8. 90

Week 3 — Day 5
1. Karen: 24, Lisa: 12
2. Jill: 21, Karen: 44
3. Jill: 27, Karen: 20
4. Karen: 27, Lisa: 9
5. Karen: 30, Lisa: 60
6. Jill: 56, Karen: 24
7. Jill: 9, Lisa: 25

Week 4 — Day 1
1. 9 m, 11 m, 30 m
2. 13 m, 58 m, 97 m
3. 20 m, 23 m, 29 m
4. 45 m, 54 m, 56 m
5. 80 m, 88 m, 108 m
6. 132 m, 146 m, 222 m
7. 801 m, 803 m, 805 m
8. 357 m, 375 m, 377 m
9. 425 m, 426 m, 462 m
10. 356 m, 365 m, 536 m

Week 4 — Day 2
1. 10 m
2. 12 m
3. 20 m
4. 100 m
5. 27 m
6. 40 m
7. 60 m
8. 120 m
9. 28 m
10. 33 m
11. 32 m
12. 44 m

Week 4 — Day 3
1. 6
2. 4
3. 9
4. 11
5. 12
6. 10
7. 9
8. 8
9. 7
10. 6
11. 12
12. 9
13. 11
14. 12

Week 4 — Day 4
1. 20 mm
2. 40 cm
3. 70 mm
4. 420 m
5. 280 m
6. 317 cm
7. 300 cm
8. 50 cm
9. 271 m
10. 500 cm
11. 50 cm
12. 400 m

Week 4 — Day 5
1. 70 mm
2. 80 mm
3. 130 mm
4. 63 mm
5. 70 mm
6. 170 mm
7. 488 mm
8. 584 mm
9. 305 mm
10. 190 mm
11. 200 mm
12. 707 mm

Week 5 — Day 1
1. 4
2. 2
3. 4
4. 3
5. 9
6. 12
7. 9
8. 9
9. 12
10. 2
11. 3
12. 5
13. 4
14. 10

Week 5 — Day 2
1. 24 cm
2. 9 cm
3. 28 cm
4. 44 cm
5. 15 cm
6. 27 cm
7. 30 cm
8. 36 cm
9. 40 cm
10. 50 cm
11. 30 cm
12. 24 cm

Week 5 — Day 3
1. 79
2. 392
3. 194
4. 152
5. 158
6. 23
7. 148
8. 323
9. 684
10. 43
11. 57
12. 531
13. 700
14. 40

Week 5 — Day 4
1. £10
2. £12
3. £12
4. £8
5. £6
6. £24
7. £22
8. £36
9. £4
10. £7

Week 5 — Day 5
1. 14p
2. 21p
3. 46p
4. 53p
5. 73p
6. 42p
7. 70p
8. 46p

Week 6 — Day 1
1. 95p
2. 70p
3. 25p
4. 65p
5. 42p
6. 24p
7. 82p
8. 59p
9. 71p
10. 89p
11. 67p
12. 38p

Week 6 — Day 2
1. 4 people
2. 10 people
3. 11 people
4. 7 people
5. 9 people
6. 7 people

Week 6 — Day 3
1. 30 missions
2. 10 missions
3. 12 missions
4. 16 missions
5. 18 missions
6. 18 missions

Week 6 — Day 4
1. 24
2. 40
3. 28
4. 46
5. 56
6. 148
7. 104
8. 126
9. 136
10. 192

Week 6 — Day 5

1.
Horses	●
Snakes	●●
Dogs	○○○○

2.
Dogs	●●●●
Hens	○○○○○
Cats	●●

3.
Cats	●●●
Lizards	◐
Birds	●●●◑

4.
Rabbits	○○○○
Dogs	●◑
Mice	●●◑

5.
Cats	●●
Horses	●◑
Dogs	○○○◑

Week 7 — Day 1
1. <
2. <
3. <
4. >
5. >
6. <
7. >
8. >
9. >
10. <
11. >
12. <

Week 7 — Day 2
1. 6
2. 70
3. 10
4. 400
5. 200
6. 8
7. 50
8. 300
9. 50
10. 9
11. 400
12. 700
13. 60
14. 3

Week 7 — Day 3
1. True
2. False
3. True
4. True
5. False
6. False
7. False
8. True
9. True
10. False
11. False
12. True

Week 7 — Day 4
1. 100 g
2. 50 g
3. 150 g
4. 210 g
5. 280 g
6. 260 g

Week 7 — Day 5
1. 9
2. 26
3. 25
4. 36
5. 15
6. 12
7. 97
8. 83

Week 8 — Day 1
1. 4
2. 5
3. 90
4. 7
5. 25
6. 14

Week 8 — Day 2
1. 100 cm
2. 120 cm
3. 140 cm
4. 70 cm
5. 40 cm
6. 156 cm
7. 182 cm
8. 148 cm

Week 8 — Day 3
1. 14
2. 26
3. 31
4. 18
5. 80
6. 10

Week 8 — Day 4
1. 631 + 82 = 713
2. 850 + 54 = 904
3. 754 + 60 = 814
4. 922 + 75 = 997
5. 881 + 93 = 974
6. 720 + 98 = 818
7. 775 + 53 = 828
8. 876 + 94 = 970

Week 8 — Day 5
1. 8 pupils
2. 10 pupils
3. 17 pupils
4. 14 pupils
5. 16 pupils
6. 25 pupils
7. 16 pupils
8. 12 pupils

Week 9 — Day 1
1. 10
2. 8
3. 4
4. 7
5. 8
6. 7
7. 11
8. 9
9. 13
10. 15
11. 20
12. 22
13. 20
14. 28

Week 9 — Day 2
1. 9
2. 7
3. 6
4. 11
5. 8
6. 12
7. 9
8. 7

Week 9 — Day 3
1. £18
2. £36
3. £140
4. £100
5. £70
6. £90
7. £100
8. £66
9. £45
10. £68

Week 9 — Day 4
1. 5 minutes 30 seconds
2. 2 minutes 10 seconds
3. 5 minutes 45 seconds
4. 8 minutes 15 seconds
5. 1 minute 36 seconds
6. 0 minutes 53 seconds
7. 9 minutes 55 seconds

Week 9 — Day 5
1. 60 km
2. 60 km
3. 210 km
4. 120 km
5. 75 km
6. 52 km
7. 72 km

Week 10 — Day 1
1. 16
2. 24
3. 8
4. 24
5. 16
6. 8
7. 36
8. 56
9. 48
10. 12
11. 8
12. 9
13. 12
14. 11

Week 10 — Day 2
1. 0, **8**, **16**, 24
2. **16**, 24, **32**, 40
3. 40, **48**, **56**, 64
4. 64, **72**, 80, **88**
5. **8**, **16**, **24**, 32
6. **24**, 32, **40**, 48
7. **48**, **56**, 64, **72**
8. 56, **64**, **72**, 80
9. **32**, **40**, **48**, 56
10. **72**, **80**, 88, **96**

Week 10 — Day 3
1. 80 people
2. 20 people
3. 61 people
4. 48 people
5. 29 people
6. 46 people
7. 102 people
8. 105 people

Week 10 — Day 4
1. 74
2. 48
3. 60
4. 4
5. 240
6. 15
7. 8
8. 131

Week 10 — Day 5
1. Aaman: £0.30, Bianca: £7.95
2. Aaman: £5.20, Bianca: £2.10
3. Aaman: £6.45, Bianca: £6.05
4. Aaman: £3.00, Bianca: £4.25
5. Aaman: £4.10, Bianca: £5.45
6. Aaman: £4.70, Bianca: £9.35

Week 11 — Day 1
1. 185, 511, 518
2. 592, 950, 959
3. 201, 210, 271
4. 418, 478, 874
5. 622, 634, 643
6. 131, 133, 331
7. 179, 197, 719
8. 846, 864, 886
9. 307, 703, 730
10. 118, 181, 811
11. 268, 286, 628
12. 512, 521, 522

Week 11 — Day 2
1. 111, 121
2. 91, 691
3. 483, 883
4. 342, 482
5. 888, 904
6. 483, 603
7. 218, 236
8. 441, 601
9. 943, 967
10. 227, 289
11. 155, 205
12. 296, 352

Week 11 — Day 3
1. $\frac{1}{6}$
2. $\frac{1}{5}$
3. $\frac{1}{8}$
4. $\frac{1}{5}$
5. $\frac{1}{4}$
6. $\frac{1}{3}$
7. $\frac{1}{2}$
8. $\frac{1}{4}$
9. $\frac{1}{6}$
10. $\frac{1}{7}$

Week 11 — Day 4
1. 10
2. 60
3. 30
4. 33
5. 45
6. 32
7. 60
8. 50
9. 64
10. 18
11. 50
12. 48

Week 11 — Day 5

1.

	Boys	Girls
Art	26	37
Drama	13	21
Music	66	51

2.

	Boys	Girls
Art	64	29
Drama	37	45
Music	22	38

3.

	Boys	Girls
Art	37	53
Drama	65	35
Music	80	49

4.

	Boys	Girls
Art	17	30
Drama	55	35
Music	22	15

5.

	Boys	Girls
Art	34	16
Drama	14	18
Music	56	66

6.

	Boys	Girls
Art	39	52
Drama	11	26
Music	55	42

Week 12 — Day 1
1. $\frac{5}{10}$
2. $\frac{4}{10}$
3. $\frac{6}{10}$
4. $\frac{8}{10}$
5. $\frac{3}{10}$
6. $\frac{7}{10}$

Week 12 — Day 2
1. 8
2. 7
3. 9
4. 10
5. 5
6. 6
7. 8
8. 4
9. 9
10. 8
11. 7
12. 12
13. 24
14. 12

Week 12 — Day 3

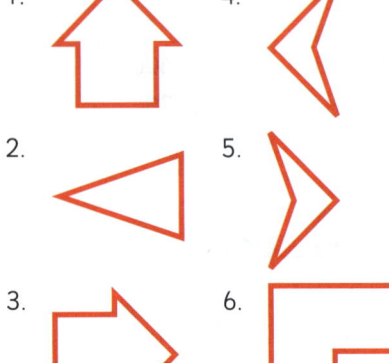

Week 12 — Day 4
1. 8 days
2. 9 days
3. 11 days
4. 8 days
5. 12 days
6. 9 days
7. 7 days
8. 6 days
9. 12 days
10. 9 days

Week 12 — Day 5
1. Striped shapes: $\frac{4}{5}$
   Striped circles: $\frac{2}{5}$
2. Circles: $\frac{3}{6}$ or $\frac{1}{2}$
   Spotted shapes: $\frac{2}{6}$ or $\frac{1}{3}$
3. Four-sided shapes: $\frac{3}{7}$
   Striped triangles: $\frac{2}{7}$
4. Triangles: $\frac{4}{8}$ or $\frac{1}{2}$
   Spotted shapes: $\frac{5}{8}$